Text and illustrations © Reverend Liz England 2023

Bibleadventuresteddyanddolly@gmail.com

Published by Dancing Waves Books

ISBN 978-1-7392421-1-4

First published 2023

All rights reserved

The author asserts the moral right to be identified as the author of this work

Christmas Bible Adventures

Teddy the Baptiser	3
Dolly and the Special Song	9
Teddy and the Difficult Question	15
Teddy the Innkeeper	19
Teddy and the Angels	27
Teddy and Dolly and the Shiny New Star	33
Dolly Follows the Star	39
Teddy and Dolly and the Blessing	45
How to use these stories	50
Where are these Bible stories?	52

Teddy the Baptiser

Do you see the light?

Are your eyes open?

Do you know what to look for?

When the light is there in the darkness, it is easy to see the light, isn't it?

And sometimes God asks us to point others to the light.

And that was Teddy's job.

And he didn't mind hard work.

Teddy had to help everyone get ready.

Ready for the light. Hooray!

And this special light had been talked about by very clever people many years ago. So everyone had been waiting a long, long time. And this special light was nearly here, but not quite yet. So Teddy had to keep working hard!

And some people thought Teddy was a bit strange because he liked a lot of different things. But we all like different things don't we?

Teddy liked to eat honey and he also liked to eat bugs!
Teddy liked wearing furry clothing and would wrap a big belt around his middle! Hooray!
What do you like to eat and wear?
Do you like the same things as Teddy?

Teddy stood knee high in the river and told everyone,
'Come and be baptised and say sorry for the wrong things you have done. A special light will be arriving soon. Get your hearts ready as you will be changed! My job is to point you to this light.'

Teddy's knees were getting wet, but he was telling the truth.

Then you'll never guess what happened.

The Light, who Teddy was waiting for, appeared at the river.

And Teddy knew straight away that this was the Light.

The Light was called Jesus.

And Jesus said, 'Will you baptise me Teddy?' And Teddy bowed and said, 'No, I cannot baptise you as you are amazing, you must baptise me instead!' But Jesus insisted and Teddy quickly threw water over Jesus, baptising him. And then the most fantastic thing happened after that. A grey bird appeared and seemed to rest on the head of Jesus. Wow!

And they all heard this loud voice from the sky. The voice wasn't Teddy's voice and it wasn't Jesus' voice, it was different voice. And the voice said, 'This is my Son, chosen

and loved, the joy of my life.'

Well, what a fantastic thing to say and to hear!

Teddy was amazed!

And after that when people asked Teddy if Jesus was the Light they had all been waiting for Teddy smiled and nodded. 'Yes', Teddy said, 'Jesus is the one, the true Light. The Light of the world!'

Do you see the Light?

Are your eyes open?

Do you know what to look for?

When the Light is there in the darkness
it is easy to see the Light, isn't it?

Dolly and the Special Song

Dolly was happy.

Dolly was so very, very happy.

What do you do when you are happy?
Well, Dolly danced!

What had made Dolly so very happy?
Well, what do you think?

I'm not sure you would believe it, you see, a visitor had appeared out of nowhere. And not just any visitor, an amazing, but also quite ordinary looking, angel! And at first the angel had surprised Dolly.

Can you do a surprised face!

And then secondly the angel had told Dolly some brilliant news.
The news was about a special baby who was going to be born...and Dolly

was being asked to help out. Dolly was being asked by the angel to be a helper and do some amazing and holy work for God.

The angel also said that this baby would be a King, and a Saviour and be a bit like a superhero!

Dolly was very happy with this news, but also a little scared. Her knees were shaking.

But do you know what? Dolly took a moment to think very carefully. And Dolly made a decision. And it was a great decision!

Dolly said Yes to the angel and Yes to God. She wanted to be God's helper and look after the baby King.

Hooray!

Dolly was so happy that she danced again and also sang this special song.

"Almighty God, you are amazing!
My whole heart knows how brilliant you are!
I am so happy and glad with what you have done.
From now on everyone will call me Happy!"

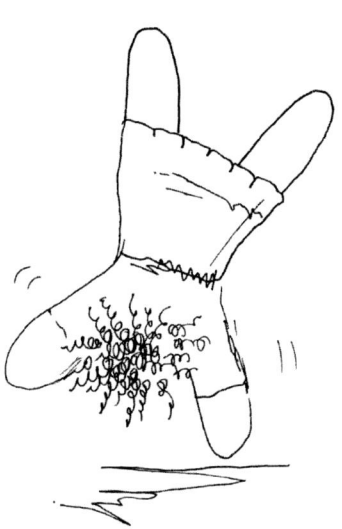

Dolly did some spinning and carried on singing.

"Amazing God you are kind to me and love me.
I will dance and sing with joy, I will twirl and spin around and around in praise, for you are the most wonderful God ever in the whole world!!"

Dolly tapped her feet and swung her arms at the same time!

Dolly carried on her song:

"You choose the weak and small to do your holy work. You feed the hungry with yummy food and keep all of your promises.

I praise you with everything I have, from my nodding head to my wriggly toes, for you are amazing! Wonderful God, I love you!"

Dolly finished her song and finished her dance, and went off to find her friend so she could tell her the news.

14

Teddy and the Difficult Question

Teddy always tried to be kind. He also always thought carefully about any decisions he had to make.

Teddy had made a decision about his friend Dolly. He had decided she was lovely and holy and he had decided he wanted to be her friend forever!

Does anyone else have a lovely friend?

But one day Dolly asked him a very difficult question. Dolly needed his help to look after a special baby. Teddy had a quick think about it, and he decided the best thing would be not to help Dolly and instead to never see her again or be her friend!

Oh dear! poor Teddy, poor Dolly.

Does that sound like the right decision?
Then they will both be sad, wont they!?
But do you know what happened next?

Teddy went to sleep and had a holy dream.
Teddy dreamt that God was telling him to help Dolly as the baby was going to be a baby King! A special baby who would do amazing things and say amazing things and would help all of the world find peace! Wow!

Teddy heard in the dream that God wanted Dolly and Teddy to look after this baby for God. And that they must call the baby Jesus, as this means 'God rescues us' and this is what the baby would do!

What an amazing dream!
Have you had any amazing dreams?

Teddy woke up! Oh my, he needed to tell Dolly about his dream as soon as possible. He quickly got his shoes on and ran to Dolly's house.
As soon as Dolly opened the door Teddy started to speak...

'Yes, I'll help you look after the baby and I want to be your friend forever. And we must call the baby Jesus,' Teddy continued - he was a bit out of breath from all the running!

Dolly smiled. A lovely holy smile.
For she knew that Teddy had made
the right decision.

Teddy the Innkeeper

Teddy closed the door.

Creeakkkk! Bang! Click, click went the locks.

Business was finished for the day, the shop was now shut.

You see, Teddy was the owner of an inn. And an inn was like a shop, but you could also stay there and sleep over if you wanted to, as well as buy some yummy food to eat. Have you ever stayed in an inn or something like an inn?

Teddy had welcomed eight guests today to his inn and the inn was now full. Today Teddy had smiled, been kind, carried bags and fed rumbling tummies. But all of that was over for the day, and Teddy was tired and a bit grumpy.

Do you ever feel grumpy?

Sometimes we all do.

Teddy sniffed as he tided the last bits of food and drink, he possibly had a cold coming. That made him feel even more grumpy! Suddenly, there was a knock at the door.

Knock, knock.

It wasn't a very loud knock at first but then, because Teddy ignored it, the knock got louder and more persistent.

Teddy looked at his watch. It was nearly midnight – who could be calling at this time of night? And as the knocking grew louder Teddy started to worry about his guests fast asleep upstairs, so he decided to open the door.

Click, click went the locks. Creak went the door. Teddy peered around the frame. And there, in the darkness stood a man, a woman and a donkey. And the woman was sitting on the donkey and had a very big, pregnant tummy.

They all looked very tired, especially the donkey!

Teddy's mouth opened wide and he was about to speak when the man whispered, 'Do you have any room for us to stay in your inn?'

Teddy was surprised! Teddy realised his mouth was still open and he closed it. But Teddy managed to get himself together and tell the travellers the truth… 'I have no room, all my rooms are full. Sorry'. Teddy WAS sorry as he was kind.

Then the man told Teddy that they had tried all of the other places and there was no room to stay at any of them. The man said that Teddy's inn was the last place they could try.

At that point the woman made a loud noise and wriggled uncomfortably, the donkey joined in with the moaning. The man and Teddy looked at the woman and the man said 'My wife is about to have a baby and needs somewhere to rest.'

Teddy had to think quickly - the woman was in pain.
Teddy remembered the building at the back of his shop.

It was where some of the animals lived but it would be better than nothing!

So Teddy grabbed some left over bread rolls and a half eaten carrot and went outside, closed the door behind him, then beckoned the family to follow him. The donkey was a little reluctant but the half eaten carrot encouraged the donkey to move. They all went around the inn and Teddy unlocked the small, dark, stone shed at the back, tucked away behind a large fig tree.

'Baa,' a sheep said as they entered the dark space and as their eyes adjusted they saw some clean hay and a space to lay down.

The donkey neighed and after the woman had managed to struggle and get off the animal, and was now gently lying on the straw, the donkey wandered over to a trough to munch on some of the food left for the animals.

The woman groaned again.

Teddy knew it was time for her to have her baby.

So, Teddy handed the bread rolls to the man who smiled in thanks and then Teddy quietly made his way out, gently closing the door behind him, Teddy hoped the family would be able to see in the darkness of the building enough to be able to do what they needed to do.

Teddy sighed. It is good to help people and be kind, Teddy thought. And as Teddy stood outside he noticed it was lighter and brighter than it had been before.

Teddy looked up into the sky, a bit confused at now being able to see clearly, and there, in the night sky, he saw a new, bright and twinkling star had appeared out of nowhere.

And the star was amazingly shining directly on to his shed where the new family were!

Teddy nodded and smiled.

'Oh good,' Teddy thought, 'at least now they will have some light.'

Teddy and the Angels

Sheep, sheep, sheep, sheep everywhere! Sheep on the hills, sheep in the fields, sheep munching grass. Teddy liked sheep, but he sometimes didn't like so many sheep around all of the time!

Teddy was cold and damp sitting on a hill with the other shepherds and lots of sheep. It was dark now the night was starting and it was going to be a cold one. Teddy held his coat more tightly around himself. He knew he'd have to stay outside all night to keep watch on his sheep.

There were stars in the sky and Teddy reckoned that for every sheep there must be a star. As Teddy gazed at the night sky, he saw a few stars were twinkling brighter than some of the other stars and some of them were getting bigger! Teddy rubbed his eyes and looked again, and the other shepherds were looking too. Some of the sheep had even turned to look in amazement with what was happening in the sky.

What was it that was lighting up the sky?

The dark night sky was becoming brighter and brighter and it was not the sunshine making it bright this time. No, it was the light of a different kind. The stars Teddy thought were there had instead become angels – bright, white and yellow, or rainbow coloured, shining angels, wow!

Thousands of angels filled the sky and Teddy rubbed his eyes again in amazement. They were real! They were really here and they were all singing! A wondrous beautiful song praising, 'Glory be to God and peace to all on earth.'

Teddy and the other shepherds looked at each other in amazement. The sheep also looked surprised.

Then one angel told them some amazing news: 'Today in Bethlehem a baby has been born.'

And if that wasn't amazing enough the angel then said, 'This baby is very special – this baby will save us all. This baby is the Messiah, the King, the special one.'

Then the angel told them where the baby with his mummy and daddy would be found.

The angels then finished their message and just carried on singing their praising songs so beautifully it sounded like the best choir Teddy had ever heard.

The sheep also enjoyed the angel's song.

What a sight! Teddy knew he would never see such a sight again. Teddy knew he must listen to the angel's message.

And when the angels had gone back to their heaven home, Teddy and the other shepherds ran off to find Jesus the baby and his mum and dad.

Afterwards they were so excited they told the story about Jesus the special baby and the amazing, singing angels to everyone who would listen, to make sure this story would always be remembered.

Teddy and Dolly and the Shiny New Star

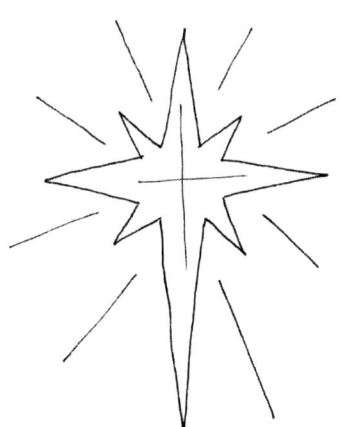

Suddenly a star appeared! And this was no ordinary star. It was brighter and shinier than any stars Dolly had seen before!

There in the night sky there was a new bright shiny star, bigger than the other stars. Dolly rubbed her eyes, but when she opened her eyes again, it was still there. She couldn't quite believe it! It hadn't been there before, but it definitely was there now!

'I know what I'll do,' Dolly said, 'I'll go and ask Teddy if he can also see It.' So off she ran to Teddy's house. Round the corner, up the hill, along the path and past the big olive tree.

'Dolly!' Teddy exclaimed as he opened the door to Dolly's loud knock. Dolly reached out for Teddy's hand and said, 'Come with me to see the bestest star ever!' Teddy nodded and followed Dolly into the night and they both went around the big olive tree again, along the path, and then at the top of the hill turned to look into the dark night sky.

'What do you see?' Dolly said. Teddy's eyes widened and his mouth opened. Teddy was surprised and amazed!

Can you do a surprised face?

He pointed at the bright star and said, 'That is the biggest brightest star I've ever seen! I love it!' Teddy was very pleased that Dolly had told him about the new star.

And do you know what?

As they stood there gazing, the star started to move across the sky and somehow got even bigger! Oh my! Then it seemed to stop, suddenly, over a place not far away from where Dolly and Teddy were standing!

And then an even more amazing thing happened! The star shone so brightly that the light from the star made one of the houses on the ground also shine brightly.

Oh my!

And Dolly looked at Teddy, and Teddy looked at Dolly.
And they both nodded to each other.
They knew what they must do.

They set off to find the star-shining house!

You see, they both knew that where the star had stopped, wherever that was, that beneath the shining star there had to be something very special!

And they couldn't wait to see what that was!

38

Dolly Follows the Star

Dolly was very clever. She was so clever she could write interesting stories, do complicated maths and ride a camel! Those are very clever things. Can you do clever things too?

But, the most clever thing that Dolly did was to study the stars. Dolly loved the stars more than anything else, she loved their shininess, their twinkling and the patterns the stars made in the sky.

A long time ago Dolly learnt that a new star was going to appear and it would be the brightest of all the bright stars! And when this star appeared it would tell them that a new King had been born. And some of Dolly's not so clever friends said this star would never appear, but clever and wise Dolly and her wise friends knew it was true, as they had studied the stars so much that it had to be right!

Dolly spotted it first and ran to tell the others.

She told her wise friends and then she had to also tell the camels.

"The star has appeared!" She exclaimed. The star, the bright star. A king has been born!! A leader who will look after and care for us all. Yippee. Dolly did a spontaneous dance and the camels joined in with some hoof tapping moves!

What do you think Dolly and the camels looked like when they danced? Can you dance?

They knew they all had to follow this bright star as soon as possible. They set off, with the bright star clearly in front of them. They went to the palace first. Of course King Herod would know where the new King was! But, King Herod didn't know.

And when he heard about the new baby King he became very jealous and very angry. Can you do an angry face?

But just as quickly he smiled instead! Can you do a smiling face instead?

King Herod smiled as he'd decided to trick Dolly and pretend. Sadly he had meanness in his heart and wanted to harm the new baby king. Oh no! Thankfully, God made sure King Herod never found out where the baby was so the new baby was kept safe. Hooray!

Wise Dolly and her clever friends set off again on their journey.

Eventually the star rose and stopped directly above a small house. Dolly and her friends knew this was the place. It was smaller and dirtier than they thought it would be, it seemed to be where animals lived and Dolly noticed it smelt a bit funny. Can you hold your nose?
It definitely didn't look like a palace.

However, Dolly and her friends left the camels chewing on some nearby grass and went towards the open door. Dolly peered inside. This was definitely the right place.

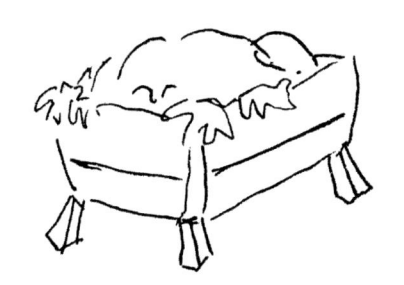

As, there in the light, lay a tiny baby. His tired mum was dozing and his dad was gazing at the child in amazement. There was a sheep nearby that was pausing every so often from her munching to also stare at the child.

Everything seemed at peace and right in the world just at that moment.

Mary the mum looked up, saw Dolly and her friends and smiled. Joseph the dad welcomed them all into their small room.

"This is Jesus", Joseph said.

Dolly and the wise friends were amazed by this special baby Jesus, so they fell on their knees in adoration and worship! They gave gifts of shiny gold, perfume frankincense and oily myrrh.

Outside the camels also knelt in adoration.

It really was a special baby. And they knew God had led them there with the new bright star!

And even though the little baby was not wearing a crown, Dolly and her friends were so clever that they knew that this was the King who would save the world.

Teddy and Dolly and the Blessing

Teddy and Dolly had been waiting, waiting, waiting, a long, long time. And sometimes waiting was very difficult to do.

Do you ever have to wait?
What do you have to wait for?
Waiting is hard, isn't it?

You see, Teddy and Dolly had been given a promise by God. That they would see the actual King and the Saviour of Israel, and the answer to their prayers, before the end of their life, before they died.

Teddy and Dolly had been praying for a very long time. Both of them had been carefully praying for their neighbours, their town and their country of Israel. All of the people in Israel needed prayer. In fact, they still do!

Do you sometimes pray?
Teddy and Dolly prayed a lot.

But, you'll never believe what happened next!

Teddy and Dolly were in the temple and Teddy was blessing all of the babies and suddenly Teddy took a baby called Jesus into his arms to bless him.

And Teddy knew.
He knew straight away.

And tears filled his eyes, and joy filled his heart, and the holy spirit reassured him, that indeed this was the one!

Teddy was holding the baby King, the one who was going to rescue the people.

The one who would indeed be the Saviour, the helper of Israel and the world, and was the answer to his and Dolly's prayers!

Teddy blessed baby Jesus and praised God saying: 'Thank you God, I am now at peace as my prayers have been answered. With my own eyes I've seen the one you promised, now everyone can see. A light to all and glory for our country, Israel.'

The baby's parents were amazed and surprised with what Teddy was saying.

Can you do a surprised face?

Yes, they would have looked just like that.

Teddy then blessed the parents, and said, 'This child will show the sadness and happiness of many and will be misunderstood and rejected. But this Jesus, the rescuer, will also encourage people to be honest and reveal who they really are and who they are supposed to be.'

It was Dolly's turn to speak up now. Dolly was known by many people for her truthfulness when she spoke. Dolly was now very old and often worshipped day and night in the temple, praising and praying.

When Dolly spotted Jesus she knew this child would be the helper of her town and country. She knew this child was the answer to her prayers and many other people's prayers. Hooray!

So Dolly danced and sang, lifting her hands above her head and praising God. Alleluia!

Later, when Teddy and Dolly went home they both had a big smile on their face.

The day had finally arrived.
The peace of God was in their hearts.
Their waiting was over.

How to use these stories

These stories are to be used individually, in one-to-ones or in any group or service that you can imagine! Tell them and repeat them anywhere. I always hope they will be rewarding to the reader and the listeners.

You will need a 'teddy' and a 'dolly' – size, colour, character doesn't matter; I've used knitted ones that church members have made for me, cardboard ones, drawn ones, ones from charity shops... If you are doing these stories regularly then I'd suggest you use the same Teddy and Dolly as I find children and adults get used to the characters.

I have also told these stories (at a baptism with 300 people) with a presentation using a screen. This worked well due to the size of the congregation. They have also been successfully used in all-age services, collective worship as well as at Teddy Bear Picnic events.

There are sometimes other characters where other toys can be used. I have found that knitted eight inch toy dolls and teddies work the best.

These Teddy and Dolly adventures are best read out loud and as slowly as possible. Take your time. Pause for effect or for the more emotional parts as it will take a time for the audience to take in what is being said.

I have aimed to print the stories clearly so you can use them directly to tell each story.

Do let me know how you get on and which other stories you would find useful to be told in this way - bibleadventuresteddyanddolly@gmail.com

Where are these Bible stories?

Teddy the Baptiser	p.3	Matthew 3 v 1-17
		Mark 1 v 1-11
		Luke 3 v 1-22
		John 1 v 1-34
Dolly and the Special Song	p.9	Luke 1 v 26-56
Teddy and the Difficult Question	p.15	Matthew 1 v 18-25
Teddy the Innkeeper	p.19	Luke 2 v 1-7
Teddy and the Angels	p.27	Luke 2 v 8-20
Teddy and Dolly and the Shiny New Star	p.33	Matthew 2 v 2, 9-10
Dolly Follows the Star	p.39	Matthew 2 v 1-12
Teddy and Dolly and the Blessing	p.45	Luke 2 v 21-40

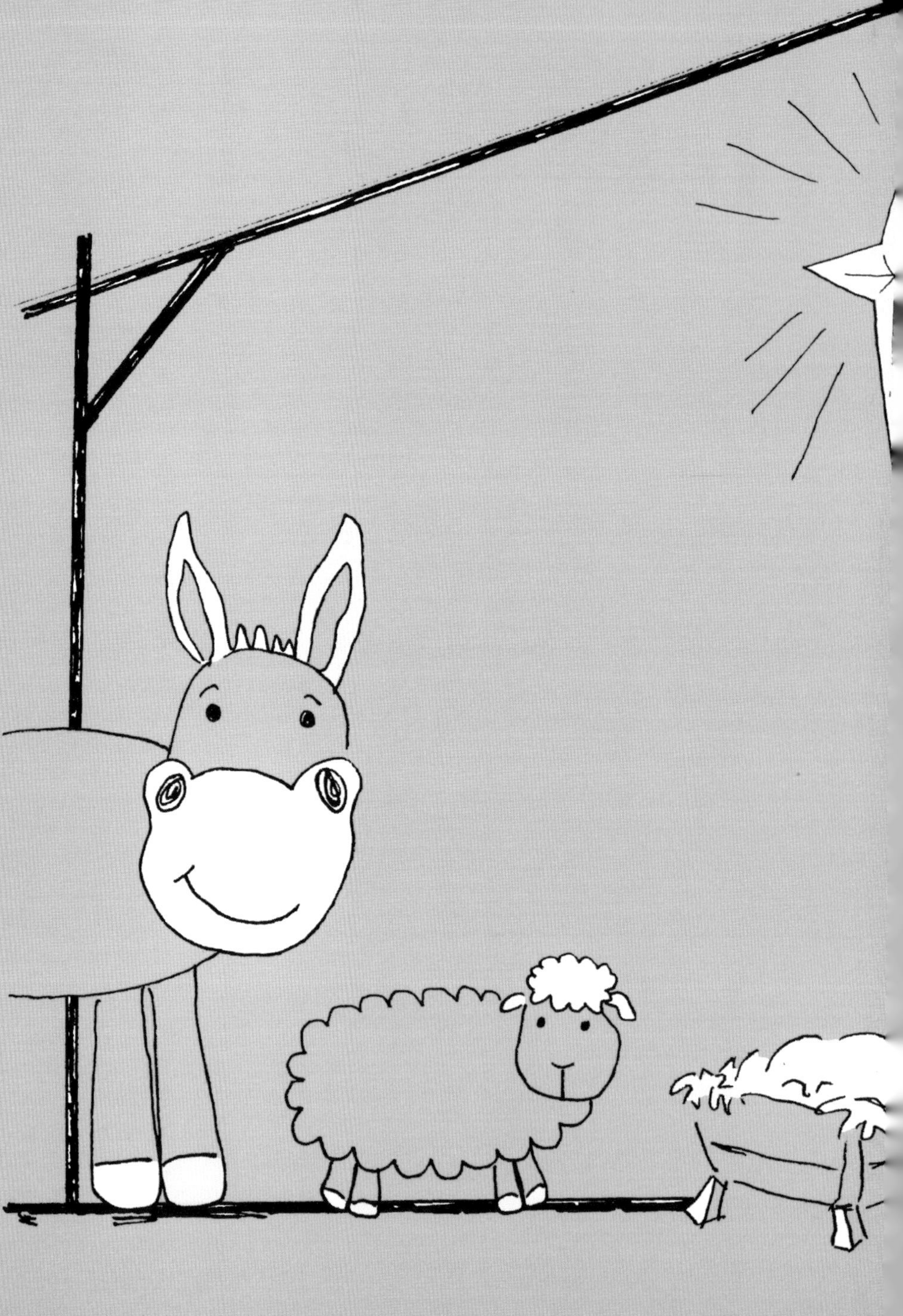